To Baby Feeley,
Anxiously awaiting your arrival.
Can't wait to welcome you to your loving family.
Lots of love from,
Granny & Peter

A Week Ago Cat

A Week Ago Cat ~First Edition~ Copyright © 2006 ~ Janet Hayward Burnham

ISBN: 0-9740743-5-7

Printed in China

Inquiries should be addressed to: My Little Jessie Press, P.O. Box 529, Bethel, Vermont 05032   www.mylittlejessiepress.com

This book is dedicated to:

Readers

Bryan
Bryce
Cassie
Jade
Kiel
Lexie
Lisa
Mariah
Megan
Zachary
Ms. Haines 5/6 class
    at The Bethel Elem. School

Proofreaders

Clare
Hilary
Kristen

To dear Cold Corner Writers,
Meg and Fran, who believed
in my poetry before I did.

And always to George.

WIND DRAGON

Today the wind
Is scouring the air,
Full angry
Full charge
Full rumbling,
Rolling
Rushing
Ranting.
I can feel
The house quake
Under my feet.

At full tilt
I hear it snuffling
Along the foundation stones.
Leaning against the north wall,
Making it creak,
Seeing if it will still stand.
And then...
In a streaming
Tail-pounding rage,
Whipping out
Across the land.

THE FROG

It's my
Considered opinion
That a frog is
Not too wise,
That there's
Not much
Happening
Behind
Those Great Green Eyes.
Do you suppose
He's fried
His brain
Sitting in the sun?
Or has
He cracked
His noggin

On the bottom,
Is that
The thing
He's done?
Because
The bullfrog
In my pond
Has the
Most peculiar habit,
He sits
All day
On a lily pad
And calls
Himself
A RABBIT!

Where up there
Do they keep the snow?
Is it in barrels and boxes...
Does anyone know?
Are there cupboards and chests full
Up there in the sky?
And just how do they keep it
Anchored on high?

Are there attics and sheds
And cellars and crates
Waiting for snowdrop calendar dates?
If you should discover
Just where it might be,
Be sure to put in
A quick call to me.

Right field's a puddle
Left is a lake
Home is the Caspian Sea,
But we played
Some ball
In a half-spring thaw,
Tom Glennon,
Ann Fenny
And me.
There were others
Of course
And they're
All hoarse
With throats
As red as the sun.
And
Tom's in bed
With a wicked
Stuffed head
And Annie's
A hundred and one.
I've got a nose

That drips six quarts,
And mom's got
Me slathered
With goo.
I hack and I cough
I sneeze and I wheeze,
I take an aspirin
Or two.
Still—
It's not
All bad
I'm not
A bit sad,
A real good
Game is the reason,
Because
I, Sally Lou,
Slammin' Sally
To you,
Hit the first
Homerun
Of the season!

The Ice Clickers

his morning
In April
Is a
Clicking ice
Morning.
There are
Thin skins
Of white lace
Icing the puddles.
Bill and I
Clickity Clack Crack 'em
All the way down the hill,
This April
In the morning.

And then, he winks at me

My grandpa
Has a fondness
For grandma's
Molasses cookies,
That's how
He says it.
He also has
A mustache.
He says
He grew it
Back when
He first

Met grandma
And found out about
Her molasses cookies.
When he talks
Like that,
Grandma gets
All afluster.
He says
He grew it
" 'specially "
As a molasses
Cookie duster.

As it used to Be

When
My grandpa
Was a young man,
He used
To farm
With horses.
Horses
To drag the plow,
And horses
To pull
The rick,
And rake,
And wagon.
So, sometimes,
He thinks
Like that.
Like yesterday
We saw a car
Without a hubcap.
"Oops,"
My grandpa said,
"She threw a shoe!"

Because
Zoe and I forgot
To take a can
When we went
To dig some worms...
And before
We reached
The fishin' hole,
It commenced
To rain...
Next,
Mama
Did the laundry
And she did fume and shout...
Because
We put
Those worms
In our pockets
And forgot to take them out!

In Grandma's
November dooryard
There's a great
And flowing tree.
The wind shakes
From it
Golden whips
And skinny leaves
For a carpet
On the ground.
Grandma says

It's her
Daughter tree,
The willow,
Because
She planted it herself.
She carried it
On her lap
Over the mountain
In a coffee can
In the old Ford truck.

A WINDING WIND

There's a winding wind out yonder
That twists the leaves off trees
That wraps the flag around the pole
That scatters clouds with ease
I hear its blathering laughter
Skittering through the air,
I hear it snap the laundry
Then turn twisters in my hair.
It's swept the sky completely clear
There's not a wisp of white
All the clouds are hiding-out
They've had a windy fright.
I bend into the swirling wind
It yanks my clothes around
It tries to sail me skyward
It wants me off the ground!

In the deep of winter
My ears are lonesome
Behind windows shut
To the tong tong tong
Of the old tower clock
Rolling out the passing hours
Across the lawns of town.
My ears are lonesome
For the chip chip chatter
Whirr and trill
Of birds gossiping in the trees

Of hummingbird wars.
My ears are lonesome
For the chirps and thumps and whine
Of insects conducting
Sales and service in the grass.
My ears are lonesome
For the rattle and wrap and whistle
Of leaves when
The wind skins past.

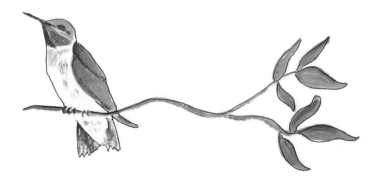

It was only
My own jeans jacket
Hanging on my own closet door
That scared me plenty
One dark night...
Until Grandpa came
And switched on the light,
And told me how
He himself had been scared
By an old tweed suit
Pinned to a clothesline
In a neighbor's dark yard,
When he was nearly eight,
And mostly quite brave.
And he said,
It was really quite common
As far as he knew,
To sometimes be scared,
When the light was just right,
By everyday clothes.

EVERYDAY

CLOTHES

A WEEK AGO CAT

It was a week ago yesterday
A Tuesday, I think,
When I happened to see
A cat dressed in pink.
She wore a fine collar
Of intricate lace
Caught up with a pin
To keep it in place.
On her paws she wore
Boots of leather and silk
Embroidered with roses
And flowers of that ilk.
But the hat on her head
Was the best thing of all.
It was velvet and ribbons
And several feet tall.
Attached to the top
Was a pot on a string

That wiggled and jiggled
And started to sing.
There were cheeses and blintzes
All around in a row
And a good bread pudding
Rolled from catnip dough.
She skated on by me,
This fancy dressed cat,
She rolled down the sidewalk
Simply eating her hat.
The next time I see
That cat come my way,
I'll try to stop her
And have something to say.
We'll speak of the weather
Of time and the sea...
And if I'm lucky,
She'll ask me to tea.

In Joneses Wood

Half an hour
Of dusting snow
Outlined
Trees and rocks
And thin paths
Through Joneses wood.
"Deer?" I asked.
"Of a sort,"
My Grandpa smiled,
"Dear John
And David
And Ann Marie,
Mrs Joneses kids,"
He said.

"That's the land
Of spies and scouts
Of Merlin
And of magic.
It's the way
To Sherwood
And Robin Hood
To Oz
And Camelot
For Ann Marie Guinevere
And David Arthur
And of course
John Lancelot."

Previous Appearances

Wind Dragon	Cricket	March 1988
As It Used To Be	Cricket	May 1989
The Ice Clickers	Cricket	April 1990
Grandma's Other Child	Cricket	November 1990
Thaw Ball	Cricket	April 1994
Everyday Clothes	Cricket	October 1994
My Ears Are Lonesome	Cricket	February 2001
A Winding Wind	Spider	November 2005